The Dauber Wings

The Dauber Wings

Theodore Worozbyt

Dream Horse Press
California

Library of Congress Cataloging-in-Publication Data:

Worozbyt, Theodore
The Dauber Wings

p. cm

ISBN 978-0-9777182-2-1
1. Poetry

10 9 8 7 6 5 4 3 2 1

First Edition

Cover: "Pieces of Red 5" by Cheryl D. McClure
http://www.cherylmcclure.com

Acknowledgments

Acknowledgment is gratefully given to the following magazines, where poems in this book, sometimes in slightly different versions, first appeared:

Anthology of Magazine Verse and Yearbook of American Poetry: "Canteen" (originally published in *Kansas Quarterly*)
Beloit Poetry Journal: "Her Thoughts"
Carolina Quarterly: "Okra"
Crazyhorse: "Fingertips"
Image: "Coming on Christmas" and "Winter Songs"
Kenyon Review: "Past Naming"
New England Review: "No Traveller," "runne softly, till I end my Song," and "Sadness"
National Poetry Review: "Tell the Time"
North American Review: "Corn," "Outside," and "The Yellow Sheets"
Ploughshares: "Scarecrow"
Poetry: "Chess" and "Neighborhood Light," February 1989, "Northern Lights" and "A Unified Theory of Light," August 1990, "Mollusk," May 1991, "Surviving Tongue" and "Visitors," June 1991, "The Guitar," August 1994.
Poetry Daily: "Scarecrow"
Prairie Schooner: "An Entire Body of Reasons," "How It Was," and "The Extra Room"
Smartish Pace: "Inside" and "Garden"
Southern Review: "No Difference Between Things of This World"
turnrow: "Elegy"
Verse Daily: "Garden," "Neighborhood Light," and "Tell the Time"

I also wish to thank the Alabama Council on the Arts, the Georgia Council for the Arts, the National Endowment for the Arts and the Graduate Council of the University of Alabama for their generous financial support during the completion of this book.

"No Difference Between Things of This World" is dedicated to E. Thomas Stuart.

"Elegy" is for Kirk Kline, 1960-1977.

Contents

I

II

III

IV

I

Past Naming

Now what do I call you? Pisser in the Empty Handy Coffee Can,
Liner Upper of Chisels, Old-Country Fireball Tomato Man?
I have not talked with you for so long, Grandfather
Clock with a Picture of a Bluebird in the Glass.

Pierogi Pirate Possum Gitchie Head of the Table Hero
where now is your refusal
to talk about wars and silver
stars? Where is it? the Ukrainian you wouldn't speak, the Polish?

Your mother cooked the schquatki, you climbed the stool to watch
minced salt-fat render and disappear, the onions
deepen their color to a black caramel.
The streets in Warsaw boiled

with the dead, and the hungry enough
to be dead, and that's the way you stayed,
Slavic Cabbage-Headed God of My Unborn Life,
and that's the way I came to have you.

O Pardoner of Slugs, Hoarder of Eggshells Crushed,
Genius Numbskull Pecan-Picking Son of an Ikon,
Mr. Fingernails Dirty Unto Death
where is the green feculent stink of beans?

Benny Benny Benny,
Foiled Fisherman with a Stack
of Naked Magazines in the Laundryroom,
Wizard of Hay-Stiff Bitter Strawberries

I am your handful of blisters and lime,
and I am stepping dully with you into the weedy edges
where something rotten is more red than I imagine.
Devourer of Anything Less than Perfectly Unnamable Love,

How now can I remember a name, the name your mother gave you?

Visitors

Unlike Goya, who represented children
with adult, foretelling proportions,
most of us envision superior beings
from another world as having bodies
much like those of infants: wide
liquid eyes staring from a hairless
head, a proofing loaf of brain,
muscles atrophied by all that thinking
about nothing more than one good look
at post-war Americans.
                                        Or did they believe
we were still at it, receiving without
a thought as we know it for linear time
our most secret codes and messages,
light years out of date, but still transmitting
democracy's beacon across the black flag
of galactic space, our signal weak but riddled
with jazz riffs and torch songs and radio
theater, when we sat down at last with the blind
to imagine the dramas of our serial lives?

A rancher heard a crash in '47, distinct
from the heartbeat of thunder
pushing rain from a sky suddenly full
of possibilities.
                                A saucerful of babies
from the belly of Cassiopeia must have seemed
better to wire in as the current of an era
than a black rain of mushrooms
whistling like a scat dirge
down the belted loins of Orion,
so when the sheriff phoned the army, a full-bird
colonel released the stories of "a metal-like
substance, thin as the foil on a pack
of Lucky Strikes, a 16-pound sledgehammer

couldn't scratch; an I-beam light
as a feather, covered with symbols like ancient
hieroglyphics in violet or purple,"
and, homesick, we bought it
at every newsstand,
                              so they kept coming
year after year, as Miller and Goodman
atrophied to a few notes
our parents played downstairs
to drown out Fats and Joe Turner, as our leader
hit the mowed-down pools of green,
balls dropping with a cluck,
pitted with pure white acne.

But it wasn't long
before jazz clubs sprang up overnight
and money grinned thick from the fold
of almost every wallet, and there was always
a hot place to go with your baby
in the tube-lit neon downtown Saturday night.
Tending the urgent boom of our own,
we forgot about Babies From Another World.

So that's where I come in, at the tail end
of a slick, confident song, missing the chance
I missed by random cosmic accident, to know them
as I know the kids I went to school with,
which is to say: then, once, and iridescently.

Sadness

deceives even the closest
and most beloved reader.
Sadness listens to a pit bull
grunt, like a pig, in the rain.
Not weight, but the space
inside a mass, sadness moves
in rigid molecular patterns, is slow,
waves slowly. In its vocabulary,
O and Ah remain silent.
Without a towel nearby, sadness
never takes the luxury of a bath.
Sadness, the chummy doctor, injects
serum after serum into sunset,
but the water wakes up as
blue and enticing as ever.
Sadness says, Say me! and leaves
a small ink footprint upon official papers.
Sadness shuffles little deaths
like cards played without cash.
Sadness made this up: the house burned
with the cats and photographs, and everyone
flew to safety on translucent wings.

Coming On Christmas

Turning corners through unknown houses,
showing up with a beard, or odd clothes,
you rustle the textures of my warped sheets,
insistent, tough as fall's tomato stalks
ripped up by the roots with a dull drumroll,
scattering dirt into my shoes. Why
can't you just pull down the sashes
when frost rimes the glass? Why not patch
that rut of your guttural cough? Why do you keep
turning up stinking half-drunk? Twenty years
have taught me about loving the swell of the dead,
their rank Persian carpets and well-lit attics,
sad fireplaces nobody uses. And just because
it's coming on Christmas, no doubt you,
hidden like a bleak secret in among the rest,
think I pine for the canopied light of a Dresden
nativity scene, its cedar roof still mossy
beneath bubble lights and heavy tin strands
on a blue spruce. By now you are always
impatient for another silky box of that ribbon
candy you so coveted, another tube of green
Palmolive shaving cream for your cup
and lather brush. Wrong again, dead man.
They don't even make that goop anymore.
I looked. So go. Mumble your vast relief
to the crickets grown weary in the grass;
go whisper the dumb patois of your Slavic Russian
to the nuts thumping dumb under the pecan tree.
Explain to those brown leaves cupped on the wind
like withered hands to ears
exactly what it means to be fallen.

Chess

Eight squares squared makes
sixty-four, the years of his heart-
attacked life, a game of edges,
parallelograms, curved
only by the buttocks of the queen,
the neck of the riderless horse,
the bishop's pointy head.
Carved, tiny man, time bomb
on a board of black and white
squares, make your move
below my wavering, thoughtless hand.
How planned, how mathematical, your life!
I suck at the filter of a dead cigarette,
consider my next move,
so many possibilities, so impossible
to predict the empty passing
of a stung pawn.
I stroke my woven wool sleeve,
I mock you: your clothes are wood.
I take you, my opponent
of another color, you are mine.
I have strategies, you
are my vehicle. I can never lose!
I take you again, I threaten
to topple your sudden kingdom,
check, check, check. Look,
your rook in the quiet corner
has vanished, half your fortress
gone in a sad, quick swoop
of my germy hand. Your men are worms
and I bump them from the world
like so many numbers running off
the end of a patterned ledger page.
And the tall man in the back row, off center,
can never be had for the taking,

he is exclusive, his hands are tied
to a little chopping block, and pale
from lack of blood. I don't want him.
But you are mine, mine, a washed-clean face
that agrees every time
on the love of the Euclidean line.

No Traveller

Grief has no country.
Its boundaries do not exist.
Not a thing, but a way,
grief assumes no shape.
Grief wriggles out and clothes us.
The password that allows,
or does not allow, anyone to cross
no border, grief wouldn't dream
of anything but itself, but grief
does not sleep and does not dream.
We talk of grieving in silence.
Grief is loud, and speaks out of our ears.
Grief is never tomorrow, but today.
There is nothing to make of grief,
but everything can be made of grief.
Grief asks of itself why
there is no question.
Grief doesn't ask itself
why there is no question.
Grief is insanely, morbidly jealous,
rubbing a neck in a mirror.
Grief offers inconsolable friendship, and a job.
In leisure grief is work,
but the converse is untrue.
Grief refuses to follow a line.
Grief has no feet, and stands for nothing.
We talk of feet of clay but grief has no name.
Grief isn't hungry, but knows who is.
Grief is the shelf, where the cans are lined.
Grief is married, but has no affairs.
Grief is weak, and depended upon.
Grief keeps moving to smaller apartments.
Grief, though short, loves a parade.

No Matter

My beard dull gray and I am gray among the stars
in that ether where all my best breaths went
their separate ways to make a little cloud
of juniper and hops and utterances so clever
they landed me, a skinny pig in the shit,
coughing on a concrete stair. Grin, I grin
into the mirror and my ground down
broken teeth are brown and grimacing
no matter how tenderly my smile purses
its flattened lips, the meat on my bones
sagging in arthritic limps. Moan a little
for the camera inside my eye is what
substitutes for explanation, then all day long
I wring my hands like bells cracking
and the scum of the sun drips along my ribs.

Winter Songs

The light has gone out and the dogs lie sleeping.
The birds have finished their winter songs.
This is the time, with night come now
fully down, when I ought to draft
a calm vintage anthem of silence—
flakes of starlight wheeling too slowly
to notice beyond the clouds;
flowers still left to the year
cupping frost in their throats;
granite stones grown stubborn
in the mowed field up on the hill.
But even in this hour
a piece of glassed-in sea hums beside my chair.
Above the zebra eel a trigger fish hovering
takes blue stock of his chances.
In the red coral cave, that stowaway crab
decorates his carapace with shells.

II

How It Was

To cling to this: the tightness
of night-cooling air. Moon
on black metal. Sounds of cooking,

sounds of children fighting bedtime.
Doors louder in the darkness.
Cars purring by with a doppled *hush*.

Tree frogs and crickets, the hum
of curled blood through my ear. Moon,
a pearl crushed in cream,

blurs through prints on the glass.
No stars drift
above the city.

To cling to this: the mouth
of nothing sucking at the skin
of farthest stars, each star

tugging at the other
with its fingertip of gravity,
and every planet joined to one arc

around a fusing sun, each octagon of wax
involved with the other
in every golden hive. This one body

joined, cell by cell,
into itself. To cling to this: the world's
bright humming mass, plain

as wind, then no wind.
Then the dark, and the cold and the bedclothes, all of it
for the night, coming down.

Canteen

With rope and iron stakes, I pitch
the regulation tent, raise it
to a taut right angle of green canvas,
a tangent to the weedy square
of rocks and clay that served
as our backyard in Vinings, Georgia, in 1968.
With the collapsing spade, I scratch a hole
where my hip will lie in sleep,
comfortable, a flexing bone
protruding into earth. I lay down
the liner from your poncho,
camouflage mottled in green.
This makeshift floor weighs ounces,
smells like machine oil
under the mildew of the tent.
I gather fist-sized stones
for the circle of my fire,
sticks of pine, maple, beech,
handfuls of dry pine straw.
My canteen is full of apple juice
and I am ready to battle the mess-kit.
The tent flap folded back, I watch
the fire burn orange, then blue,
listen for crickets and tree frogs.
I think of you at Omaha Beach, my eyes
full of documentary footage,
"The World at War," "Victory at Sea."

Now what's left of bivouac
is this dulled steel canteen,
and I keep moving
to smaller apartments.
The box where I keep it
is in one home
or another.

Garden

Outside in dug soil
grubs curl, sickly
and new.

Moisture, grit and rot
turn the iron wheel, the slow
forgetting of the world.

Succulence and feculence
kiss, suck, penetrate
the other

of the other.
Waving eyeball,
fittingly

green on a green blade,
sees what, a blur
of turning worms, the monolith

of the foot undoing sun, sound
and chewing.
The voices of the dead

are smells. A hospital
of stinking geraniums
nods its blooming head.

Why wet rot?
Let it broil into dust.
Radishes swell

into globes,
scarlet, crisp
in the compact black.

Nothing but a Swell of Tenderness

It is nothing if not the tick bloodying my ear.

It is nothing if I step on the passion flower
on the gravel road down to the bog.

Into the hilled loam the wind goes.
Into the tine of the red machine
the gentle night crawler.

O my throat, in this grass, among these pines,
it seizes thirst by its own throat,
the golden pollens having nothing
but their love of light and rain.

Little time is left here
and all of the sweet decisions
have poured from my cup of honey.

All of the delicious insistence of the skin
soughing against the skin
has fallen away too slowly to have witnessed,

like a fruit pit detaching from its flesh
and catching in the dust underneath the tree.

And pity is so lovely in the morning
when the wings of the grasshoppers lie
folded soft in the dew.

And pity is so loveless when
the sun climbs the trees and flies away.

It is nothing if not the tick's head buried in my ear,
nothing but a swell of tenderness
that burns when touched.

The hour has come to pass the rake across the dirt
and smooth the beds in preparation.

Though my muscles are sore,
though my heart is like a hand too blistered to fist,
I must. No choice remains

but to make and sleek the place
where the wolf spider may cross
from the boat of the leaf into the toad's lair.

The Guitar

is an insolent hole through which I pour
the petty details of my longings.
There has never been for me
anything so beautiful, the drivel
of these attempted sounds. I want gloves
with fingernails, then nothing absolutely
would touch me. By now I am crawling
toward some Segovian fugue. Who wouldn't want
a spiraling out of memory's flexing
augmentations? Dissonance is its own
mother. Within harmonics, the fleck
of black grit resides, dormant, dominant.
The eye wanders forward toward code, coda.
And the ear cannot rest.

Elegy

The Hodaka mutters with a high throat.
Knobbies slick mud onto the street,
the Bell Star helmet yellow as a leaf.
Little Sammy drops through creek ice
to his waist and looks down, whimpers.
The pups came out, long gray grapes,
the night he locked her out and burned
a Gigi's pizza. She found a butter knife
in the yard where the zinnias strangled
in a ring of rocks, and tried it on
the sliding glass door in the dining
room. But Jackie Gleason was funny
when Alice just stood there. On Ed
Sullivan men balanced spinning plates.
Pink papers tasted sweet when
you licked the glue. The field had rocks
and at the edge blackberries. I kissed
India's tongue in the clubhouse.
She moved her long black hair.
The photo albums have disappeared.
The mountain for gears has a restaurant
now serving veal in cream and snails.
Once I ran so fast without shoes
the canes didn't cut my feet.
He made me eat it in my room
and she waited below with my dog
for him to let her back in but he didn't.
I talked to my mother from the balcony
that went around my bedroom
where the box turtles scratched the closet
and then I went to sleep in my soft bed.
The cardinal hid in the corner
until I tried to pick him up, then
exploded through that opened door.
Suzie Landcaster had long dusty
brown fingers that moved the papers
from one stack to another in the back

of the classroom, slowly, slow
and fascinating as snow coming
to a windowsill. The Coke bottle
house where she lived had no toilet
but its yard sounds green in the wind.
After the harmonicas stopped Kirk and I
left James and Harold in Niggertown.
Around candles old men had needles
in a burned house the three-legged
dog stayed away from, and we ran
down the trail from their turned heads.
Kirk makes the premix; oil blurps
into the gas tank. He shakes the bike
to slosh it, hooks a leg over and kicks
the crank. It catches. One down,
four up. I often dread the thought that
I might plunge a needle into my eye.
Station wagons don't quite turn over
in the rain. Kirk was waiting
every Friday, his face there
behind the smoked shield,
his jaw a curve of fiberglass,
when I got off the yellow bus.
The acid was free and purple
all the way through when we cut it
and swallowed. Pools of premix
burned gelatinous and blue
on the sidewalk near dawn.
At the country club with hot dogs
on buttered toasted buns I broke
my tooth on the three meter board
the first time I tried a half-gainer.
Her lips were soft as scrambled eggs.
Spareribs hurt with a broken tooth.
They slide a long way on their sides,
music still coming from the radio.

Ineluctable Fish

My password was a bruise then it changed
to the scent of burning tar settling across
a cloud of mosquitoes in the heavy dusk.
Standing in the grass with the brindle dog
I could hear dark zippers in the trees
closing up like rubber bags. The moments
in my bones began to ache, and I felt
coal barge horns compress my organs like
a rush of sweat when fever breaks.
Beyond the green door the rugs lie,
stitched ears listening through the floor,
stubbled faces bright with vegetable dyes,
raveled and shifting like burnt clouds.
The dog has a chance to run at dawn.
Otherwise his life is rope. Noon we slog
dripping drool under the sun, hooked
hand to throat. A sack of raw fish waits
every day in the same spot. On the sidewalk
a wren dissolves into a swarm of soft teeth.
The lady raking mistakes me for a policeman.

No Difference Between Things of This World

Down he runs from the yellow-jacket hill,
Down from the sound of water rushing in a rock,
Down and shattering the leaves, leaping the fallen
Trees with such light-breaking work that the ground
Bends away from his flying animal grace.

Down fly the leaves in a mid-summer wind, down
Falls the whiteness of clouds through an afternoon rain.
Down climbs the man on the ladder, down the brush
Sleeks along the line. Down come paintings when I grow
Ready enough to paint. Down slides the sun in a blaze.

Down arc the divers from their cliffs and boards, their falling forms
Cut toward abandon, coiled and clasped in the air, let them go
Into their beds with their nightmare books, into forgiving water.
Down dip my hands; I cup them at my face to drink.
Down to the blue bottom I went, and hung there, but watched.

Down island paths I will have gone, to see waves sway
Across the sun; down island paths, to breathe salt air in the saw grass;
Down the soft dust of island roads to walk with my feet bared clean
Toward the common dream of love and the spark in its hectic eyes.
Spores drift down from downy ferns, and down from pools tides move,

Leaving hermit crabs for birds to pick. Down tick the hands of the red clock
In the corner in the dark, when I let sleep choose me. Down slide
Muscles along bones. Down run the batteries, who knows where.
Down her face I tend my fingertip, to trace the map of water.
Down below the hornets' eaves the mums bloomed and dry.

Toward a darkness yet, the dauber's wings extend, assurances
Sealed into papery cells. Down my throat the scalding food
Follows, garlic browned, thin tomato broth, elbow pasta, russets diced,
Stuff my grandmother packed into my box when I left home for home.
Down lap the husbanded miles, my left hand folded on the wheel.

Down collide these fingernails with string, shaping a music to the hollow.
Down shave iron planes, the measured woods fitted with a fragrance.
Down below heaps of trophies and rope, a tool chest in another box
Hides auger bits bright in wooden cases. Down was locked
The lid then, hung with its pair of captured rip saws. The lawn

Laid down in the rain. Sheet lightning shot from builded clouds
When the priest began to read; then out, out went the lights.
The purple tent collapsed under shovels ripe with sleet,
And the ribbons got sunk with a trumpet's note into the body.
Still I send my hand to greet each misremembered shadow.

Down dropped a row of gloves, cupped chilly in salutes.
Down were laid three silver stars, the purple hearts, into Viola's dresser.
The barbed wire fence crimped down on Stella's dog, and down leapt
My grandfather into streaming gore to save his daughter's eye.
The sound of water rushing in a rock, the echo of the clover,

A splashing in the leaves, such sounds are what I might
Have said or done once. A tangled pulse of waves through air
Is the same to me as time's rupture of the light. I look down.
I wind this watch. Each chance that I need will be noticed soon.
No difference lies between the things of this world. But

He runs, he does, from the capsized field of hidden nests,
And to the ground fly leaves of light too crisply down to me
Here in this place where a desert sails across the picture
Pretending to be the sky. Through windflowers gathering
Quiet in the wind and past the monkey puzzle tree he pistons

Round the pumphouse in the brim of his dark track.
There where elephant ears dissemble the tarnished coin
Of a baby snapping turtle, and when the lone bunting's
Blue dart plunges through branches wooled with cloud,
I go with him eager to the bottom of the world's bowl.

Through the tiny orchard where the honey grows, then past
The hedge of garnet-colored roses nodding over pit bull bones,
Down along the river where echoes run green in the fallen sun,
He heaves his flanks into the hollow where ferns splay their furls.
I have come by him to the sweetwater river where the echoes run.

III

Fingertips

Then the cutworm entered the squash
and the wall refused the nail. Before
time there could not have been more
than one thought. The live-forever
in the basket unfolds pale violet
beneath a canopy of bent wire,
barely a color at the visible end.
The dog barks, a gun on the table,
nothing there. The chisels lean
from their box against the plaster.
Geodes make history the future.
Tenderness was a draught selected
so cold from the tub your eyes ached.
Bliss is someone else's father
whose glasses flash, whose stub
of cigar fogs the pink speaker
tuned down to the engine's hammer.
You can't be young alone. The grass,
not yet mown, thickens and flicks
up tiny white moths. They tap
against the rolled glass windows
like the fingertips of the dead.
The skin of a woman's belly
makes of tenderness a sad religion,
the touch of a hand, that miracle,
nearly always too late to ripen.

A Unified Theory of Light

Everything depends
on the largely abstract
elements of the human

we push into the real
world of things by an action
of the hand, the lips, the tongue.

A hand cannot move
gently enough
from one moment's touch to another.

We are not what we think
of as this body, its miles
of telegraphic nerve and vein,

its weight of marrow, pints
of plasma, balls of vitreous, aqueous humors.
We see and touch this body only

because it changes and resists
the available light. The light
is what the body isn't, and perhaps

this is reason enough
why lovemaking grows more tender
when the body

of the earth turns us
against the constant fusion of the sun,
its unending illuminations.

And by "unending" I mean
to say only that the light
beyond our reach

will outlive the dimmer spark
we perceive as ours.
But how much truth is there

to be found in reaching
for a history of things
in a universe where the one causal principle

we can ever fully know
is the uncertainty
of relations?

We can never say a star—the star
we turn away from
nightly, one unique but sharing

the same bright conversions and exchanges as the billions
of others, all bodies, rolling and quivering through
the frictive vibrations of time

toward the absolute
density of entropy—can never say a star is an event
that burns the woven cloth of space

more deeply
than this, our singularity,
when the unmeasured pulsing between two bodies

thoughtlessly joins to one motion
in the penetrated sheet of the dark,
like particle and wave coming at last together

from nowhere toward the center of this room,
like the spark, irreducible, we know
created everything.

Mollusk

Banana slugs choke the rail
garter with mucous, inconsumable.

Salt and gold and manganese
flood the sea sea scallops breathe;

a clam's one white foot moves and moves, a wave
of convulsions, the sucking O

mouthing algae continuously.
How these shells mock me!

I drown or cannot drink.
Painted snails glisten in dampness and the moon,

tracking, like constellations, a dim
mythology of absences.

Hermaphroditic sway and kiss,
all tongue and eye

and slick, perfect love.
If the dart stings, it only appears

to incite more passion. In the star-blue
gluey lick and kiss

bulbs of semen pass into wombs. No need
to touch but they do. No home but the body.

The squid pulses
salt, a jellied bloom,

hydroencephalic flower,
brain and nacreous eyeball

rolling in a blind depth where lung,
heart, and cell collapse.

Oysters clack like stones.
We heap them on the beach, the dull knife shucks

into a bowl of lemons.
Split jaws shriek a silence of pearls.

No dream can penetrate it,
the cold onliness of a joy and its purpose.

Northern Lights

When piano means soft
and plainly smooth, and to beat
means to hold

time in a pattern
of strictest beauty,
when *rubato* doesn't mean to take

but to borrow,
and every undeniable statement
asks a question

seeking a reply,
when to retard
means to make more

complex, more human, like the beating
of your heart,
and dominant is a clearly worried tone

seeking tonic, and a rest;
when development means returning
to the place where you began,

only better this time, and with more
to say, when absolute
means a music unencumbered

by the abstract
reductions of speech
and sequence means one thing worth repeating

over and over, if in a different pitch,
and when recapitulation means not
redundant monotony but a new sense

of ripening and fullness,
and coda means not the tail-end
of constraints

but the fruition of a single event
of the song,
this is when my mind comes to rest

on the slenderly muscled whiteness
of your arm, the violin cased and packed
a seaboard away

in your mother's house,
the snow falling there already without you.

An Entire Body of Reasons

Because we borrowed the tiller
from your father, bought seedlings,
pellet-lime and manure,
and planted tomatoes,
the purple and green basil,
banana peppers that brightened
to coral among the flat-leafed parsley,

because we mulched soft red clay
with newspapers and the neighbor's leaves
and kept out the vines of morning glory
so well the Better Boys and Bonnies grew
beyond our heads, a caged green firmament
bursting with ripe red giants, spending itself
over and over as we watched from the deck,

because I dipped hundreds in boiling water
and stripped their skins with a French
carbon steel knife,

because I mashed the raw pulp through a colander
and ground the jellied seeds in my sink,

because I simmered and simmered it—days went by
until the house was full of it, even in sleep—
and rolled the meat and egg and garlic
in my hands like a raw benediction,

because I had my windows down and turned
off the radio when I stopped
to check the mail coming in late
from work last night and heard the dog
barking, whimpering, howling all at once,

and because I looked at him once in the dark,
a white mongrel poodle clearly belonging to no one,
sitting at the corner of the sidewalk
unattached to the blurry imperative of anyone's front door,

I drive forward asymptotically towards a faith
in being able to make things up to the dead—everything I
love dies—and I connect
this dog to someone recently dead, forty years after Belsen...

because I hear him now in my building, outside my door
in the lit and carpeted hall, wailing undeniably
in all three voices, and it is late,
after midnight,
and I am tired,

I stand naked in the kitchen
spooning at the cold red gravy,
filling an old bowl with meatballs and bread
that I will slip beyond the door

so I can lie down again
beneath the field
mouse ticking along the joist in the attic
with a sound too hidden or feeble to hear.

Horoscope

You will be alone
for a time, and then
rediscovered by the one

who, like yourself, has waited
far too long to be happy.
Love requited utterly

will frighten you, but watch
how your secret garden
blooms into wide, green

airs. Your room
of childhood, the big carved bed, the books
await you.

All choices rest with you now.
Take what is offered, or you may lose everything,
but also remember:

the past
has truly passed. You are not the kind to live
inside memory

but so many you have loved
are gone, you can't help it; it seems natural
that sometimes

love to you means loss.
The things you can't quite believe
are wildly important

to your happiness, and there is an answer
for which you have no question. You trust, rightly,
in little, nameless acts

of kindness and of love
to calm the sad man of your frightening dreams.
Romantic by nature,

you often feel
that others around you have given up
their hearts to pursue

doubtful powers
that breed an essential loneliness.
It is difficult for anyone

to convince you
of the things you already know:
beauty in your mirror

never tells more
than the state of what you're sure, by now,
is your soul,

and your mind is much
occupied by others, their need of constancy
in your thoughts to be happy.

You suspect
you have been forsaken
for someone's idea

of who they wanted
you to be, but happily you will discover
for the first time

all over again
how wrong you are. Joy!
and you deserve it.

It's true, introspective
and hardworking as you are, that you can
know yourself too well,

but the only advice this week
is to write the letter you had forgotten
you needed to write.

By next week you'll be home
from an unexpected trip
to receive it.

IV

Surviving Tongue

What survived of *lic*, the word
for the body before
Chaucer lobbied for the dignity

of its compromising
positions and urges, is "lych gate,"
a place

for pallbearers to rest
the casket on ceremony
made concrete, if penultimate.

And, perhaps, if we squint, "licentious,"
the pedant's polysyllabic license
to look down on the flesh, Platonically,

of his Roman nose
at the idea of his or any body moving
its bowels toward anything like

the ideal. And "like,"
which is most likely the most
lively part of what

Emerson called "fossil poetry,"
that what we have is like
what this body was: like,

or some derivative, as in, Wet is like
water, or, What would
water be like if wave were like tide?

And, Yes, we love but
do you like my body making
this S against you every night,

resting inflected in the warmth
before sleep? An old body like this
body, a wordless caesura, lies between us.

But since every word
makes another, and we account for each
and every one in time, I'll say

what litanies the body likes to hear.
Let's go give ourselves a license to derive
as much plain, incomparable joy from licentiousness

as dulling nerves will allow
before the bodies so much like
these bodies we know now

pause tongue-tied on their journey.

The Yellow Sheets

The yellow sheets smell of sunlight and your dark hair.
Touching there is musical, a held pulse quickened.

The wings of bees overheard through the window,
the color of their sweetness rising through your skin,

the salt pink sea rose of you, hidden on my lips
in curls of shadow, petaled around my tongue, all

bloom undermoving with your limbs, and in your eyes, there
where times unfold and disappear,

reflects the image of wind-swelled curtains in a breath,
in silence, in our air.

Okra

Snouts from yellow blooms, they snoop
through fingered leaves, depend
from cane-thick spines.
We cannot love these tacky interlopers,
but clip some for the basket anyway.
And no matter how hard we wash them
it is always the same. Sliced,
they fall from limp paper towels
to the black iron skillet with a thick hiss.
Sizzling renders slime, the mass
gargles heavy bubbles.
Like a crawling memory of slugs,
this disturbs us. But recipes
are commitment: the moment steam gives way
to sticky glaze, we dump
the whole mess in the soup pot,
spatter the bright red bath.

Corn

Friend, what does it mean when my wife buys corn,
frozen corn, canned corn, corn in a little pouch
to boil and slit, economy corn, family-sized corn,
yellow corn, white corn, name-brand corn;
what does it mean to find this exhaustive unbroken
spectrum of corn behind appliance and cabinet doors,
new corn appearing weekly, adding up
to more corn than my mind can bear or bourne—
another mystery, yet another, the mystery
not of corn, the tucked-in tail of a root
shooting out bleached in dark from the seed,
the slender emerald stalk reaching for giant
coulds and clouds with the glittery wave
of a burlesque pastie, a tassel of Empire silk,
but another mystery altogether separate
from the milky farm—I point to corn here
and there on a shelf and I ask
in my estranged Tiffany vernacular,
what does it mean when you buy corn
you don't and ne'er will eat? Does the soul
of Adonis still lie among the corn? Where does
old corn go, and when does it go there?
And why not ever fresh on the cob—Silver
Queen, Golden Trumpet, Candy Dandy—
to boil and slather, to strip and cream,
to leave unshucked and roast over coals
some mild summer evening on the deck?
You don't even like the smell, do you?
Outside the kitchen window there must be
a corn-jeweled glacier slowly sliding by and eating
the unmown grass, the corn must be
burying the red birds in the trees.

And I know

deeply in these moments, when the corners
of things give way to shadow, how I must

turn myself over to the shifting forces
and invisible objects which form our ideas of love.
I take my tumbler of whiskey onto the deck
where all yet remains quiet, quiet, save
the tiny clash of ice-noise like a toy piano in my glass;
and I'll do no more here than watch starlight's first kernels
tremble and sweeten the dark field stretched above me.

Her Thoughts

A plait of geodes: her thoughts, of smoke and of melons
grown from vines of pure air, are sky.
(I have named these holds of quartz and work
for the journey of a pearl along her shoulder.)

Unknown without her the coagulated dark
on muscles, droplets sliding along glaze, waste
of sheared, luxuriant years burning like coffee
in my mouth: unknown the scoop of yolk-colored light

that runs a green river through hidden tigers' eyes,
the bestial planet where my atmospheres
raise tongues from a winding sea in the whirl of breath-
making. Unknown, the anaphoras of bald-toned miseries

and their dream of a final despair. Unknown,
and unfinite, the questions dragged like sour dirges
out of puddles, the hearts corded with staves,
the dulled orchids, ratty drain-hairs leached.

Her tresses stretch on intimate damp scissors,
her sunflowers spatter the dry beaks of cardinals.
My hunger for the brightness of such knowledge
slides a blood ruby down my throat,

and these are hours I have dug from the earth
cast and moist, smelling of fresh iron.

Neighborhood Light

Like the rim of the known
universe expanding into the dark
non-edge of space,

the blurred knots
of the local clusters dragging
apart, drifting undone,

the golden arms
of each galaxy opening to the slowing
original spin,

like the loosening grip of each star
on each rotating body
revolving around its cooling center,

like the bodies themselves,
planets grinding down on imaginary
axes, each year a linear fraction longer,

like the light that pierces
the frail shell of atmosphere
on this planet, the light of dead stars,

like the expanding rim, the stars at the boundary
rushing into nothing, their light moving in,
moving out, light we'll never see,

like that light, the rays never entering
this sky, this sky a few molecules poorer
each lengthening day,

like the swell and ebb of the living
mass of species, emblems twice withdrawn
to abstraction by the reductive statistics of speech,

like the Dead Sea, the briny death
of its wet iconograph, the brilliant shapes
of crystal driftwood on its shores,

like the blind white fish of the caves,
like the song of the snail darter,
like the fish living on the edge

of the fresh, blinding hot currents
pushing into the edge
of that sea, every sea becoming that sea,

we come apart each night in the incandescent room,
untangling arms and thighs. How lovely,
the rich sweat of our finished work,

the bound salt that binds us
to the dim light thrown through the window:
starlight, moonlight, the light from this quiet street.

Outside

When you brought the pitcher
I smelled the lemons
in the water

and the sugar loosened my tongue.
The lawn was done
with its cut,

and green, and across your shoulders
your light shift hung
like a veil.

I was so thirsty in the sun.
Your feet were bare,
your lips

cool and dry. Even the liquid
in the glass became
unbearable.

Scarecrow

Last summer the Better Boys bloomed,
tiny saffron flowers going off like slow
Chinese rockets, and set their pinhead fruits.
I'd ordered a pint of ladybugs from Burpee's
catalogue and scattered their crimson clock-backs
through the furry, pungent leaves. I sat
in my resin chair, observing the light
of late afternoons move through rinsed branches.
Black-capped chickadees
slurred whistled E-notes and dove—
an abrupt hop and slip with safflower seeds
into the weeping willow.
Love apples, nightshades, *lycopersicon*
esculentum. I read their poisonous
New World histories, studied the preferences
for powdered lime and a weekly inch of rain
(one drenched season I watched ripening
crack into rheumy weeping).
I could not act against the birds,
who love the bright cardinal red
of Fireball skins, the wet mass
of seed encased in a cartwheel
of pulpy gelled flesh.
                                        I drove a stake
into the soil and wrapped the salt
marsh hay into my clothes. I made
the chest deeper, the arms more full
than mine, and stood him up at the shade end.
For eyes he had sunglasses, for ears sacking.
His fingers were my gloves.
I grew to enjoy his solitude.
Out there in the dark and light,
he never dreamed of what he was up to,
never had a thought
he didn't need. And when he came,
at last, to have a certain allure

to the thrushes and the jays,
I didn't give up, as some might,
on his stationary potentials.
Stranger things have failed to happen.
This summer a tornado two hundred
yards wide dropped a pine-framed tin garage
into our neighbor's yard, poised
to consume our house, and then
just rose over the roof and flew away.
I heard a Midwest couple on a talk show
tell how they rose into the funnel
saying goodbye. The husband said
he felt light through his closed eyes
the way a sleeper feels the dawn,
and he looked to see himself riding
"a magic carpet of air, skimming
over buildings at a good clip" until
God set him down ten feet away
from his wife on the ground, unhurt
till he sat up and got back-smashed
by a timber, breaking every rib.
They were happier now, each day
a sweetness. Yes; exactly. A sweetness.
Rooted like the smell of grass and lime.
The next morning I remembered dreaming
I placed a millet seed in someone's mouth.
Nights got longer, the scarecrow frayed;
scraps of his moldering entrails doubtless
lined the thrashers' nest. He never had
any sort of hat, so with glasses on he started
to look like the skinny blind man
who used to lean against the granite wall
of a bank across from the subway station.
I stopped weeding: the vines grew
freckled with liver-colored mold, turned
yellow as the flowers, and browned.

Still he stood guarding cages, until
my affection for him—like heat
from the earth's dirt skin—finished waning.
I confess my relief at his uselessness.
I dragged him, one Indian summer day,
and all the tattered papery leaf-litter
he overlooked in mocking silence, out of that
manicured plot and down to the curb,
pocketing my shades and gloves.
I went inside and laid a pointless fire.
We weren't here when the tornado
lifted. We saw it from the freeway.
I was bringing my wife home
to Tuscaloosa from the Atlanta airport.
She was driving because she gets carsick.
I looked out my window and we stopped
under an overpass. The funnel was black
but its edges were glittering like dust
made out of glass, and the sight of it
flattened the sky. Out west, her nephew
was dying from stage IV neuroblastoma.
I'd stayed home to feed the cats and the turtle.
After I didn't light the fire I went out
on second thought to unbutton
my old white shirt from the scarecrow.
I thought I'd snip it into rags
and wax the cars. Instead I packed
some more books to carry over
to my new apartment. The moon
was orange and huge when I came in
to pick her up. Five miles up inside
the sky, she must have
watched the moon as she flew.
The birds were here first, my wife said.
I drove dead east, watching
little but my hands on the wheel.

The Extra Room

When they divorced he went back, while she was in Memphis,
to the house. He would feed the cats and move the things
leftover. Instead of moving the things he brushed the old boys
daily, overfed them, and took a clipping from the zebrina.

The clipping rooted and he bought a green plastic basket
to fill with sterile mix. The clipping grew and he clipped it.
The basket soon filled and he was mildly pleased
with his secret. Perhaps he might reveal this harmless crime,

this furtive propagation, in a letter, a subtle and winning aside.
It would be a story they might savor in the years to come.
She moved in November, and for some reason the opportunity
to mention the zebrina didn't materialize. Seattle, she wrote, was misty.

The pot got root-bound, so he sheared the vines
and repotted, but he was left with handfuls of clippings
secreting their clear gel on the table, an imposing vitality.
He remembered zebrina leaves littering the deck after a rain,

purple and silver-striped for days. He bought more pots and mix
at the home center, transplanted. When he moved to take a better
position in a larger town, he took the pots of zebrina.
There were twenty-three of varying sizes, most made of clay.

It happened that the house he rented had a room he didn't use.
The zebrinas had grown lanky during the move, and his sense
of probity urged him to construct cherry-stained boxes
to preserve the necessary pile of new clippings. When he ran out

of window aprons he built raised beds for the floor, hung
a grid of stained dowels six inches below the ceiling and ran brass
brackets along the walls. In the center he placed a slate-topped
table facing his chair. Now, he thought, he would write home.

Inside

Here, in the woods, cutting
lawns, the dogs

languid on the cement apron
porch, their leads

a tangle of red wire, I cut
the motor and listen

to heat-silence tick away
into the renewed

chatter of cardinals diving
toward the feeder

two stories above my head.
The sweat turns

my t-shirt to a washrag,
funnels down

my baked face. Time now
to go in, where

there's air, where I make sugar
and lemons into

the drink I have been
these three years

too lonely even to wish
to taste again.

Tell the Time

The contour of a bedsheet, a fabric on a fabric
touched coolly, touched softly,
changed or swept of crumbs and

tobacco shreds with a light
queasing pass of the palm.
A quiet now counting itself like

measures before thunder.
One mississippi, two. Touched beneath
the wavering memory of a bald moon.

Result, and residue, we are.
Touched and in time touched, but not in time.
Slowly in the outside air

sparks lift themselves to blink above the lawn.
They cannot tell the summer of your hour
but they coded and told.

Should we mount a conversation
and its fond and glacial impasse, its passed sting?
The movement of the brush along the line

is what I know—at the forest's edge—of color.
Sanded dabs and coats are interspersed
with the ringing of a muscled telephone.

You have told me if, and when and once,
and the trees, the stars went on focusing the sky
through an amber droplet falling

from the white saw cut in the white pine.
As if they always, star and tree, root and moon,
were falling, will have

been made to fall.
A solstice, an equinox blend.
God would lean into a prismed cloud if God

were what the handyman believed in.
I have forgotten, I have been forgetting something
that once seemed too important

to remark. Love in time is time—love is time in time.
I cannot surely answer
forgetfulness with a silken vow.

How often had the promise been made
that we would go like climbers among the small
green attainments of radishes and flowers.

I ushered a mud wasp out the front door—
and a form of pain or kindness was left behind,
as if these were not the feeding hours

of the *cardinalis cardinalis*
and then not a brick laid into his soil,
unseeable but still, *be still,*

interrupting the uniformed grass.

runne softly, till I end my Song

It was the river running slowly and my seeing it.
It was the turtles in their boxes, and the racer on the ground.
It was the long since past come lastly again in every leaf and ripple.
The trout circled slowly in the pool that I yet might make a witness to.
Then it was the sun becoming brass in the sorrow of my hopes.
And who but I should have known there, in the fleet
Hollow of the painterly light what was to come.
What was to come was this time of praise.

It was the shining black excellence of the coat.
It was the bulk and bulse of muscle disappearing.
It was the fan of dark hair making the transparent move.
The lobelias flamed at the edge of the sand.
They were called cardinal flowers then
But I cannot call them out now by their names, for
Their red is like no other color I have known.
Even the end of love is not so brilliantly plumed.

It was the wind, and the branches shining with spider threads.
It was the wild hard zygote of the beauty berry.
O it was the river, the water, the smoothing sound.
The barges ferried their glittering mounds of anthracite.
The fishermen sped their glassy boats beyond the shoal.
The waves slapped in and in, brushing the silt into a cloud.
Honeysuckles numbed the air with their moist throats
And tooth-shaped bits of milky quartz lay scattered along the ground.

It was the smell of vagrant rot in the boxwoods.
It rang in the clustered bloodshot of the nandina.
Low and long I sang in the green combing of the grass.
It was the trees and the stars fallen away beneath you.
It was the white pines that rose oldly to feather the air.
It was the gaping hole in the holly, and the failed gold-
Speckled aucubas, the constant impatiens in the wet shade,
The wrongness of the bunting's name, the brown fungal ring in the lawn.

The blue heron broke the air, and sliced the churned river.
O purple scar hung beneath the orbit of your breast!
I smelled the stink of fear in my own mouth.
It was the cold pumped air and the thin heated blankets I laid over you.
Low I sang in the green ward, in praise of your light sleep.
It was your blood, moving surely in its hidden ways.
Dog of my heart, be still and faithful as you will.
O yes, it was the river that has gone. And it was you,

Who have risen clearly as the current flows,
Who crossed two continents, erasing the chalk of hours.
It was the brick-small plot where I laid the bright body of the cardinal.
It was the dish on the ground where he lit to die, and it was the weeping
Willow where bronze bells swayed below the ruby-throated hummingbirds.
The madwoman living in the Crepe Myrtle tree wore black every summer day.
Her small folded paper kept penciled trace of the time.
I asked her how she could rake leaves in this heat; she pointed

To herself and whispered *I'm not wearing a bra.*
It was the road her son died on running a load of bootleg beer.
It was four in some morning she woke to find a stunning cold in her bed.
It was her husband's heart that sent her screaming to the window.
It was the first of many sirens, and then across the street
It was the particular cancer only infants contract.
It was the mass of white flowers like a basement fungus
Sponged round the tiny vessel where he lay, Sean.
It was the cold wide river whispering its poison.

It was the carp tossed up on the path, the textile of flies.
It was a foxtail slitted into the thicket, it was bees;
It was the wood-ticks' crawl to seek the inner ear,
And the great heron's glide alone over the flow.
It was the river took me down beside the sea.
I held you in that buoyant water as if you were bodiless;
I held your long flanks, your undulant knees, the forms
Of your wild hair, and it was there where I tasted the curing brine.

But it is the river, dark, brown, thick as melted wax, I return to,
Stamping the frost-blind clover and walking the drop of the bank.
The rockface bristles with club moss; catkins tip oak branches,
Telling too early spring. It was the river running slowly
And my seeing it. It was the turtles in their boxes and the racer
Stirring black and yellow on the ground. But it was loveliness, too,
And grace, when I watched you walking toward me in the grass,
When the sun cast down its veil of light, golden around your shoulders,
When your sundress bloomed a pale thousand blossoms, each too delicate to touch.

www.ingramcontent.com/pod-product-compliance
Lightning Source LLC
LaVergne TN
LVHW050941080826
845145LV00004B/1360

* 9 7 8 0 9 7 7 7 1 8 2 2 1 *